CW00606970

REFLECTING WATERS

Edited by

Heather Killingray

First published in Great Britain in 2002 by
POETRY NOW
Remus House,
Coltsfoot Drive,
Peterborough, PE2 9JX
Telephone (01733) 898101
Fax (01733) 313524

HB ISBN 0 75432 782 5
SB ISBN 0 75432 783 3

FOREWORD

Although we are a nation of poets we are accused of not reading poetry, or buying poetry books. After many years of listening to the incessant gripes of poetry publishers, I can only assume that the books they publish, in general, are books that most people do not want to read.

Poetry should not be obscure, introverted, and as cryptic as a crossword puzzle: it is the poet's duty to reach out and embrace the world.

The world owes the poet nothing and we should not be expected to dig and delve into a rambling discourse searching for some inner meaning.

The reason we write poetry (and almost all of us do) is because we want to communicate: an ideal; an idea; or a specific feeling. Poetry is as essential in communication, as a letter; a radio; a telephone, and the main criterion for selecting the poems in this anthology is very simple: they communicate.

CONTENTS

I CLOSED MY EYES AND FOUND YOU

So close to me I couldn't see
  The way things truly were
Beyond my dreams, my memory
My life, my world, my destiny
Somehow she found the best in me
  I found these things in her

Was getting by and biding time
  Was alright on my own
I didn't mind which way I went
Or how my nights and days were spent
Until this someone Heaven-sent
  Brought happiness unknown

And so your world how does it feel
  What beauty does surround you?
When all my thoughts have turned to peace
Past tears of sorrow all deceased
From all my chains I've been released
  There's freedom all around you

Below the ground, above the skies
The tides, the moon, sunset, sunrise
The birds themselves sing lullabies
  For Heaven's creatures crowned you

A something lives and never dies
The stories written in your eyes
  For my own eyes I closed
And met you where my sanctuary lies
The greatest zenith in the skies
For suddenly to my surprise
My world woke up before sunrise I closed
  I closed my eyes and found you.

Sparky

1

A LIFE BONUS

True friends are thin on the ground,
May take years before one is found,
Always there in times of trouble,
When life bursts as a soap bubble,
If tears rain face because love strays
Be there too, it works both ways.

Listen while friend pours from heart
Worrying problems to impart,
You may suggest but not to stress
She will learn not to acquiesce
All the time, for full happiness
To another's bossiness.

Good friend is stairway to sky
Escalating your down to high,
Birth, anniversary, dating,
One firm friend for celebrating
Acquaintances not a minus
My friend is my life's bonus.

Hilary Jill Robson

MY DEAR SISTER VELMA

When we were young 'Look after your little sister,' they said,
And somehow since then it's always been in the back of my head,
If I could help you now you know I would,
You are the sister that's always been good.
If I could change places I would gladly do this,
You've had all the bad breaks that I seemed to miss.
I'll love you forever and I'm not far away
If you want to talk or have things you need to say.
I pray the Lord be with you and keep you in His care,
And remember dear sister, I'll always be there,
For blood is thicker than water, but this we already know,
Dear sister I hope you know I think the world of you.
Just you and I remain now from our dear family
So may the love I offer help to set you free,
Free from pain and worry, free from toil and strife,
You are a special person, I'm glad you share my life.

Joyce Hammond

DAVID'S POEM

Streaks of red,
against a pale blue sky.
The sun is your smile,
the breeze your sigh.

I've lost a good friend,
a friendship strong and true.
But I have the memories,
of times spent with you.

A real good man,
with a heart of gold.
You should have been around,
till you were wrinkly and old.

The good Lord gives,
then He takes away.
But you shouldn't have gone,
you should have stayed.

Streaks of red,
against a pale blue sky.
The sun is your smile,
the breeze your sigh.

Deanna L Dixon

GRANDAD

When he needed me, I was not there.
It must have seemed no one cared.
I feel so guilty, I don't know why.
I just don't see why he had to die.

He walked alone, I was not there,
He died alone and no one cared,
All except me and his family too.
They really loved him, I know that's true.

It wasn't my fault, I couldn't be there,
But not because I didn't care.
Please forgive me, I hope you do,
Listen Grandad, we all loved you.

Andrew Brian Zipfell

MY SOLDIER

My thoughts are with you all the time,
I love you very much,
I thought I would drop you a line,
I do hope we keep in touch.

You are my very best friend,
Also my dearest love,
I will trust you till the end,
Until we meet again.

You are a soldier you had to go and fight,
For your country and what is right
God is good and I hope you will be back home to Blighty, and to me.

May Ward

WHAT YOU MEAN TO ME

I feel so lucky to have you in my life,
Even though I haven't seen you for a while,
Your friendly words I hear when you call,
Never fail to make me smile.

You always know just when to call,
When I'm upset, alone or feeling sad,
Your gently, soothing words you speak,
Make me realise it's not all that bad.

Whenever I've got a problem,
That no one else would understand,
I pick up the phone and give you a call,
My guardian angel is always on hand.

You turn my tears of sadness,
Into tears of laughter once more,
I'd put my life in your hands and give my world to you,
After all that's what friends are for.

So I dedicate this poem to you,
To tell you how dear you are to me,
You're my one true friend in this world,
You're the person that makes me, *me!*

Claire Smith

HEARTS OF GOLD

'Who's that coming up the stairs?' I cried.
I had left the door open wide
To assure him he was always welcome,
he entered the room where I reside,
Who? The tinker of all trades - my brother.

What's that on your list of things to do?
Some I put aside and some I haven't a clue.
My favourite pastime is verse or poetry
And he finishes it with beautifully written calligraphy.
Who? The tinker of all trades - my brother.

At solving jigsaws he is second to none,
He sets it all up for me - the border done
But when he comes back, I haven't moved
And so he gets me an easier one.
Who? The tinker of all trades - my brother.

I wake up and find it's Saturday
The day he and his wife visit his sister,
We decided last week, if it's fine,
We would paint the ramp for Micky, my scooter
Who? The tinker of all trades - my brother.

I ask at Sainsbury's for Mike's buns
And they always know who I mean
They are really called Almond Slices
And he has the nuts off my ones.
Who? The tinker of all trades - my brother.

For a treat, he takes me for a ride.
As I'm disabled, the cockpit I share
For the very best of Surrey's views
With the very best of Surrey's crews.
Who? The tinker of all trades - my brother - God bless him.

Rosemary Smith

FOSSIL
(Dedicated to my mate, Anna on the occasion of her 40th Birthday)

It really must be awful
Once you reach the big 4-0
Apparently your hair goes grey
And things begin to go.

Your teeth begin to yellow,
Your reflexes get slower,
And e-by-gum, there's worse to come -
Your boobs start hanging lower.

You get great bags beneath your eyes
Your waistline starts to thicken,
Your sex life hits an all-time low -
Forget the term 'a quick 'un'!

You'll stand out at the disco -
You'll be the oldest there -
And when you dance you'll wonder why
The folk all stop and stare.

Okay, so I don't mean all this,
Come on - as if I would!
(Besides, I like you as a mate
Cos you make me look good!)

Tracey Kay Dean

TEDDY BEARS

My teddies are all shapes and sizes,
Holding beauty within.
Some are fluffy and fat,
Others tatty and thin.

Some are love-worn and threadbare,
Their fur long since gone.
Some need lots of attention,
Others demand little or none.

But one gives more than others
Her hugs warm, tender and true.
She's my bestest, favourite teddy.
And yes, it happens it's you!

Jean Caldwell

WHAT SPELLS FRIENDSHIP?

F   for fame that comes and goes, but a *friend* is there, forever close.
R   for riches that can end, but never the help of a faithful *friend.*
I   for injuries and pain, but a *friend* supports till you're well again.
E   for enemies' scornful traits, but a *friend* encourages always.
N   for need when nights seem long,
     but a *friend* is there like a morning song.
D   for days when skies are grey, but a *friend* says
     'Sunshine's on its way.'
S   for sorrow with its stress,
     but a *friend* gives strength till the pain is less.
H   for happiness that comes from having cheerful, loving chums.
I   is for invitation to sail through life with a friendship crew.
P   for prayers for all those *friends* who'll be there till my voyage ends.

The Captain of Life's sea will choose
The time and tide for the greatest cruise
On SS Friendship: climb aboard;
When your name is called by the Living Lord.

Marion Payton

PATCH
(For Shirley)

For many long years, you her companion were;
Her family and friends gave you their trust;
Because so close to her, you knew her thoughts;
Your love, devoted; and your counsel, just;
You strayed not from her side, by night or day,
On outings, or at home; at rest, or play.

You were her knight at arms, there by her side;
You fought her battles, and upheld her worth;
To be with her was all you wanted, and
To serve her was your dearest wish on Earth;
You were her friend, and her protector true;
The love you felt for her, she felt for you.

Candy, Sasha, and Scoobie, the cat,
Were your good friends; you played, and all loved that.
Handsome were you, with white and orange fur;
You barked a welcome to the cat's soft purr.
Now in Heaven's fields and gardens free you roam,
With loving thoughts of friends in your first home.

Patricia Marston

WHAT WAS THAT?

Did you hear a little noise?
Was it something meant for me?
I saw your ears suddenly twitch
I cannot hear you see
Was it someone passing
Or the click of the latch on the gate?
Are you awaiting a knock on the door
As your reaction I await?
You are a faithful little friend
You alert me to every sound
Life has been much better
Since you have been around
What would I do without you?
I cannot cope alone
I am sure you know you are doing good
As my love for you has grown
You never ask for any reward
Just the pat of my hand
I know when you look with your loving eyes
That you understand
We get along together
I cuddle and hold you near
You are always ready and willing to work
You know I cannot hear.

Evelyn A Evans

SHAYNE

Long ago I befriended a boy
Who was hurt and in great pain,
I took him to the hospital
His pale cheeks turned to flame.

A simple gesture, which began
A friendship long and true
He said I simply had to ask
Anything he would do.

This grateful boy, became a man
Tall and strong and kind,
My age has gathered and my
Strength has long been left behind.

He carries bags I cannot lift,
He does my household chores,
Two lives entwined quite happily
Our friendship's deep because . . .

My kindness was a rarity
His gratefulness ran deep
Throughout our lives we've cherished
The friendship we two keep.

Eighteen years is 'distance'
On things that can be measured
But eighteen years is precious
When friendship can be treasured.

Linda Cooper

Linda Coop

Safety + freedom is the best thing
in my life. Jealousy is a nightmare!
I had a Mitral Valve Prolapse due to my
running to save my life. from this
man.

MY ROSE OF KELVINGROVE
(Linda my love . . .)

How sweet you were when first I saw you all those years ago,
My heart was taken over all at once and I knew that you would stay
with me all through life,
And here you are for all that you have been through,
still so radiantly beautiful and still my Rose of Kelvingrove,
oh how I love you.

There are so many who admire you and I am
so proud to be the one who has seen you
blossom into the most beautiful and caring heart
that I have ever known.

Long may you blossom my love,
My Rose of Kelvingrove.

Holding the key to your heart has been the most
privileged thing in life for me.

Francis Joseph Lawton

PETER, MY FRIEND

I had a true friend once several years ago
And I loved him so much, I do miss him so.
All his life he had a unique way
Of knowing exactly every word I would say,
He could not speak to me like humans do
But his eyes looked at me and said that he knew.
He would sit at my side, I would stroke his head
And each night he slept at the side of my bed,
Every day I would take him out for a walk
And while I was walking I would quietly talk.
I expect people thought I was going mad
But they did not know he was all that I had.
In the summer he would chase the cats away
He wouldn't have hurt them he just loved to play,
He was someone that I could tell my troubles to
And he'd sit and listen then bark 'What can I do?'
He never moaned when things went wrong
He just wagged his tail, that said 'Now come along
You've always got me, don't worry about it.'
But then he grew old and he wasn't so fit
Our walks got shorter and very slow
All those years I'd had him and watched him grow
Now I have to carry him up the stairs at night,
But his heart gave out and he lost the fight
He would never have hurt me or caused me pain
Oh how I wish he was alive again
Yes, he was my true friend and companion too
Could anyone wish for more . . . would you?

Gladys Baillie

A LIFETIME OF FRIENDSHIP

My mum was the best friend I ever had.
She would laugh and cry with me.
We loved each other very much,
And we loved a pot of tea.
She knew the answer to every plea.
We had no choice with food or clothes.
We all would eat the same.
But our clothes were clean and plain.
All with embroidered hems.
Thursday was her cooking day,
She would bake the bread and cakes.
I had all the bowls to finish off,
before they were washed,
She talked to my first boyfriend,
And vetted him for me.
Not that I would ever listen.
Although she was the best friend I had.
My brother and my sisters were younger than me.
I would stay at home from school,
And be a little mother.
Other times I cooked and cleaned.
And make it look much better.

Heather Ann Breadnam

BEST FRIENDS

We enter this world in our birthday suit
People close, hold us, and say we look cute
We grow up and travel through time
These are; childhood, adolescence, old age, all fine

Of these times, you're lucky if you find
Friends that are close, someone you don't mind
Throughout life, you will always meet
Friends so close, they are so neat

These friends, joined like bricks in a wall
Something goes wrong, like dominoes they fall
These aren't friends; you want to have close
Those that stick by you, are needed the most

These I call my very *best friends*
There by your side, always making amends
At a shout, through the thick and thin
Whatever you've done, is never a sin

Never leaving your side
Ultimately, nothing to hide
People living their lives, have never had a *best friend*
At their side, their troubles they tend

Unique to you, they're always there
Helping each other, as one, but a pair
If you have a *best friend*, an ally at your side
They're there to appreciate, believe in and confide

Laying down their lives, only for you
However you appeal, or tell them not to
Special kind of people, they're sure to be
Respect, a prize, a bond for eternity

Best friends, make amends

N L Coles

PUSSY-WHITE PAWS

My faithful, much loved pussy cat -
Most certainly my greatest friend.
All say he is a 'gift from God'
His loyalty knows no end.

Now bereaved, so oft alone,
I turn to stroke his velvet head.
He gives me his so treasured paw -
His special love, soon tears are fled.

But is he only 'just a cat'?
Oh no, most surely, so much more
I often come back in sadness,
But he is always by the door.

He always knows when I need comfort
Creeps in my so lonely bed
To caress my aching heart
With his gentle, snow-white paw.

So pussy cat, I thank my God
That you are here, with all your love
Perhaps your much honoured help
Really stems from One above.

Marcella Pellow

FRIENDSHIP
(Dedicated to Dorothy Morrow for sixty years of friendship)

Friendship is a special thing
It can't be bought or sold
Friendship is a special thing
Whether we be young or old.

Friendship is a special thing
How lucky then are we
For your friendship is a special thing
Specially to me.

We have been friends
For many, many years
And that friendship has been there for you
In laughter and in tears.

Whenever you have needed it
You have only had to say
For my friendship has been there for you
On this and every day.

L E Davies

FRIENDSHIP

True friendship is the purest kind of love we ever know,
It has no limitations, can only stronger grow.
Endures when other feelings diminish, fade away,
And distance does not lessen it, once forged is there to stay.

Token friendships by the score but none that ever last,
Flourish still they start to bore, or sorrows choose to cast
Their gloom upon the scene, and very soon they disappear
As if they'd never been.

But friends there are who pop around to see what they can do,
Enormous consolation found and such a friend are you,
No fuss or lots of useless words, a sympathetic ear
And soothing warmth which soon surrounds me
Just by being near.

Someone always there for me in times of grief or stress,
And if apart seeks for some way to ease my loneliness,
A situation hoped to last until the very end,
And when that final parting comes will still remain my friend.

Ellen Thompson

SUCKING GOBSTOPPERS

Young girls with freckled faces,
Auburn-haired school friends,
Strolling along holding hands . . .

Sucking gobstoppers . . .
Rolling them around
Monster gobstoppers, we once sucked and sucked . . .

Sucking gobstoppers I remember well . . .
Fresh colours revealed, they decreased in size,
Flavourless, washed white . . .

Lesley J Worrall

AMONG THE EMPYREAN VORTIPLANES

Focus on the sky, and the wind flow above
Watch the glint of metal from the wave riders
Always obsessively watch for the by-ways
Watching for that movement in the weird dimensions
Where increasingly the focus concerns energies
Around those craft, that flow in the contemplation.

Michael C Soper

MY NEIGHBOURS

Mary and John are good neighbours and friends
We don't make a habit of 'borrows and lends'!
For quite a while they've watched my place
They keep my house keys, just in case.
In both of them, they have my trust
I thank them lots, I know I must.
They clean the pond and feed the fish
Make sure the cats don't have a 'dish'.
I hope that they will never move
If they stay, I will approve.
Good friends and neighbours are hard to find
They are people of a 'special' kind.

Ethel Wakeford

THRU' THIS WORLD . . .

Forever, He is, our Friend -
Thru the muck an' the mad mile;
His Word and Spirit, surely mend,
His sweet Love can make us smile . . .

Jesus is, our Saviour's Name . . .
The Friend of sinners - all;
He took it, on Himself: the blame -
Died that we may hear His call
Of loving forgiveness!

He is the Forever Friend -
God our Father's Son:
He's The Shepherd, He attends
To each child, each precious one,
With His Love . . .

Forever friends, is what, 'we' are,
And thru prayer and Grace,
We shall be healed neath The Morning Star:
We shall see His Face,
In our Brothers and Sisters.

Oh forever . . . forever! Yes, forever!
Never t'part . . . for Jesus lives
Never t'leave us, forsake us - never!
His sweet Spirit, He gives
In His love.

Friends forever: You me and Him
Thru faith in the Son of God:
He is our love, and He is our hymn
As thru this world, with Grace, we plod . . .

Anon

FOREVER FRIENDS

He comes to my bedroom
He sits on a chair,
I tell him my troubles,
He really does care.

He is so very gentle
Always has a smile,
And listens attentively,
All of the while.

I've cried on his shoulder,
My tears soaked his shirt,
I know it upset him,
To see me get hurt.

One day I hugged him,
Close to my heart,
Kissed him goodbye,
For we had to part.

Stoically, silent,
He left, oh so sad.
I cried for days,
And felt so bad.

Some time later,
We met once again,
At a Sunday flea market,
In pouring rain!

Now, we're together
Forever, I swear!
Just me and my Huggy,
My adorable - Bear!

E M Eagle

ALL IS NOT LOST

We cannot be lovers,
There's too much to lose,
Too much at stake,
Too many hearts to break

We cannot be lovers,
But friendship is fine,
We'll talk, we'll smile,
That will make life worthwhile.

Joyce Walker

A FRIEND

A friend is like a precious jewel found
Within a mound of rubble, buried deep.
Unearthed and sparkling in its dull surround,
There shines a treasure that you want to keep.

Someone who listens when to talk, there's need,
Who lifts your spirits when you're feeling low
Who selflessly performs a kindly deed
Without requiring other folk to know.

Who laughs with you at life's amusing tales -
Collects you from the valley of despair
And patiently gives hope when all else fails
To show the smile of fortune waiting there.

Essential as the air you need to breathe,
The helpful hand on whom you can depend,
The therapy you certainly achieve
From all the care and comfort of a friend.

Joy Saunders

PETER (AGED FIVE) TO GRANDMA

Grandma!
Can you knit me,
A jumper that's just right,
The body not too long,
The neck not too tight.
I don't want it to my knees -
Or halfway up my chest,
Should you stop about my waist
I think that would be best.
But should you get it wrong
And it doesn't fit me right
I'll still love you Grandma
And kiss you every night.

J A Silkstone

CHEERS M'DEAR

Thank you for being my best friend
I know it isn't always easy
I babble on for hours about nothing much
But you never seem to get bored
I cry at soppy films far too much
But you never get tired of handing me the tissues
I dance madly all night long when we go out
But you never seem to get embarrassed
You are the best friend a girl could have
You care, you listen, you share,
You give great advice
You are always there for me
So this is why I have written this for you
To say thank you for putting up with me
To say thank you for being my best friend.

Lindsey Brown

NAN

To the most beautiful Nan in all the world
Your beauty and love shines forth for all to see.
In the people you touched and who knew you
For even though you're no longer here
You live in our hearts and our minds
I will never forget your wonderful smile
Or the truth and love in your greying eyes
Your ever open arms, no matter what we did wrong
And the way that when we were down you kept us strong.
You may be in the Heavens up above
But we still remember, your everlasting love
I remember the things you said I would be
And the manners and truth of life you taught me.
I'll never forget all the sacrifices you made
So to you a single rose on Mother's Day.

A M Williamson

A LIFETIME OF LOVE

The roots that you have given to me,
Are foundations created,
For my life to be.
They are precious and treasured,
And live on in my heart,
Though there are many times,
We have been apart.
Don't ever doubt,
How essential you are,
And it matters not,
How near or far.
For across the miles,
You sing to my soul,
Should you forget the words,
I'll make the song whole.

Sue Umanski

TIMELESS FRIEND

Whenever I need a word to say,
You lend an ear;
Whenever I need somewhere to stay,
Your home is near;
Whenever I just can't find my way,
You wipe my tear.

If ever I'm sad and need to cry,
Your arm's around;
If ever I've news that brings a sigh,
You hear that sound;
If ever I've failed a task to try,
You rally round.

But when I've news that brings me pleasure,
You rejoice too;
When I've a gift I wish to treasure,
You're there to view;
When I've a time of precious leisure,
You share it too.

But the greatest wonder in my heart lies -
That yours is the friendship that never dies.

Sheila E Harvey

THE ARDINGLY SIX

From their senior days, and junior school
Occasions, when they played the fool.
These six young men found they could bond
A lasting friendship they, to fond
Those past days of fun and frolic
The village pub trips, as alcoholics.
Observations of them all
Bring back great memories to recall.
Although it's rare, these days they meet
Their past school days are hard to beat.
Jimmy, Mark, Mike, Clive and Shane
All led by Adrian, with that school scheme brain.
As old Ardinian's no doubt they'll meet
One day to dwell on school day fetes.
This said, the housemasters of their day
Often called, in school chapel to pray.
Their prayers as follows, Dear God do tell
Some scheme, so help us, to expel
This loveable, dashing, vibrant mix.
Those seventy's seniors
The Ardingly Six.

E L Hannam

BE MY FRIEND

You make my heart sing
I feel like a king,
But nobody knows, what tomorrow will bring
We go round life's corners,
A big, giant bend,
Whatever it takes, please be my friend.

Paul Raine

MY MENTOR

I got a friend
Who I share my
Life

He is always
There when things
Are bright

I talk and he
Listens as I
Cry

He finds the time
To guide me
Right

He is my mentor
Cool and calm

He will be there
Till I die.

Bav Naker

SEA DANCER

A leviathan moves,
In the semi dark below.
Slowly, graceful in the deep,
Soft, sunlit shadows.

A graceful sea dancer.
That sings of the deep ocean.
Sing to us of that deep world.
Give us some notion.

Of the silver starfish.
The rainbow anemones.
Life below the ocean waves.
Dreamer of the seas.

Maria Arnott

BEAUTIFUL THINGS

Some people can see beautiful things,
though they've been blind from birth,
Still they can appreciate, Mother Earth.
With all her sensations, winds from the sea,
textures to touch, flowery scents,
warmth of the sun, Heaven sent.
Tastes of food, from around the world,
laughter of children, ringing in ears,
strange sensation, after a couple of beers.
Touch of a friend, causing physical pleasure,
descriptive tales of talented writers,
letting them know, bishops wear mitres.
The feeling, from hot and cold water springs,
and, I suspect,
many, many other things.

Danny Coleman

REMEMBERING

If you are by a lake
Throwing stones
And you throw one in a certain way
It will bounce and bounce
Across the water's surface
Sending a spray up each time.
Like memories,
getting fainter and fainter.

Until you throw another stone
And bring them all back again.

Athalia Pyzer

HEATHER, MAGNOLIA AND CHERRY BLOSSOM
AND THE GREAT WHITE SUN

Tiny, white spurts of heather
show the minuteness of the Creator's mood
Sunshine after shower
shows the completeness of His mercy.
He does not wish us to grieve forever.
The magnolia bush puts forth
Waxen flowers. The stems are strong.
So creation goes forth on its way
After so much tragedy.
Peace is dwelling in the heart
Of the cherry blossom,
Saying, 'Come to me and be healed'
Sniff in Nature's fragrance
And be still. Listen to the heart
Of the eternal, most wonderfully kind.
The great white sun
Blazes down on the Earth
Such is the holiness of God
That we cannot even look upon Him.

Ann Bradley

STREAM

Listening to the gentle, flowing noises of the stream,
I transport myself back to a time of sheer bliss,
Where my life was in harmony and I was happy.
The sun shines brightly upon my face,
To feel its warmth makes me glow,
It reminds me of a safe and tranquil place,
When my personal warmth would easily flow.

Listening to the gentle, flowing noises of the stream,
Again I am taken away - like a baby being born,
Everything seems so new and daunting,
The sunlight dances upon the water, too afraid to touch
Into its depths for it could drown
By the immense feeling that the water holds.

When at last the sun dares to dance,
The beauty is for all to see,
The world can be a wonderful place,
If we could find our own special stream.

Helen Legg

A MASTERPIECE

I woke up quite early one day in July,
The year two thousand and one.
Above, was a perfectly clear blue sky,
So I breakfasted out in the sun.

I looked and I listened, relaxing alone,
Enjoying the moment of peace,
When, there from the sky, I heard a low moan
And the sound began to increase.

A shadow spread out on the ground nearby
And the world began to go dark.
I shuddered awhile just wondering why
A spoil-sport should make his mark.

But then in an instant I understood
This unidentified noise
This moving cloud (I knew I should)
Was geese! O joy of joys!

This start to the day was one of the best.
A sight most magical!
Flapping rapidly - many abreast -
Geese - of numbers Biblical.

How wonderful! God's power brings
The knowledge and the strength
To guide the geese, with heavy wings,
To fly the country's length.

So, deep in thought, I went to work,
And travelled with the geese.
Aware that God's great handiwork
Was one huge masterpiece.

Marjorie Norton

THE FALLEN ROSE

I waited at the fallen rose
And watched the midnight dance
Where silver starlight sparkled -
Once again I'd missed my chance.

I drank the moon's reflection
From the depths of passion's lake
And felt the breeze caresses
As sighs wandered in its wake.

Kim Montia

ABERTREWEREN, BACK DOOR VIEW

On the bank beneath the trees
daffodils, dancing, weave their way
to stretch and reach towards the
distant view of other valley side,
as though the very intent and bobbing grace
could seed the faraway high horizon.
The patchwork greenery brightened, lightened
underneath the tree gloom standings
by the golden trumpeting, all attention,
leaning forward, glowing in the breeze.
Glittering green companion leaves
supporting the advance into perception,
gently apart from the crowded bramble,
yet near enough to every guardian tree
for each bright bunch to feel
the ancient security of planted
deep footings in the lee of aged rock.
Steep bank, with solitary bumblebee
creating harmonies.

Lesley Vann

MISTY

I look to the star
That shines so bright
In the darkness
Of the night
When the mist
Dries my eyes
The wind will cry
As
The clouds hurry by
My heart will smile.

Helen Owen

LOVE

Oh this sight I do behold the sunlight glistening on the snow
All these beauteous colours I behold like the rainbow,
For all these things are given from our Father God,
So man can see the way he hath trod.

For when we look upon the tree,
You see the love that God has for you and for me,
The sky, the sea, all these things God made for you and me.
The beauty is there for all to see
All the flowers that bloom in the hedgerow.

M Ackroyd

THE RIVER'S PATH

The path it turns, twists and winds
Meandering along the river's side
Through grazing fields, the river will pass
Flowering meadows and woodland dash.

Through villages it sits beside
Flows under bridges some tall and wide
Across moorland and dale it curves and tones
Rushing ever onward rambling home.

Down waterfalls it plunges clear
Over jagged rocks and pebbles steers
Tumbles through mountains, rugged and tough
It widens and deepens, shallows and ruts.

Trickles through valleys, peaceful and still
Slides around countryside and craggy hill
It tumbles and gushes, babbles and moans
Floods and rushes, but forever it roams.

The path it bends and curves much more
Through towns and cities it dives and falls
But keeps the river by its side
Companion or perhaps its guide.

Christina B Cox

SEASONS

The soul in Winter burns, smoulders
with the fiery colours of Autumn
flaming orange and raging red
contrasting the cold, black and white
the shadow and the moon
of each ghostly, lonely night
these moth dead months greying
so smothering, softening
yet still it yearns for
the clean, green of Spring awakening
reviving and refreshing
in its unceasing continuum towards
the dawning, mellow yellow warm
of the spiriting sun of Summer
that sets the sleeping butterfly to flight.

Fiona Clark

SOLITUDE

There's a solitude on an empty beach,
The corners of my soul it's bound to reach.
The feel of the sand beneath my feet,
The cool waves lapping a soothing treat.
A gentle breeze blowing the hair from my face,
The cobwebs of my mind disappear without trace.
Patterns in the sand as the constant waves flow,
On their ceaseless journeys to and fro.
Skeins of seaweed lie along the strand,
None of their patterns ever pre-planned.
Memories evoked of years gone by,
Of rockpools, sandcastles and kites to fly.
The cool evening air and the setting sun,
Telling us another day over, another day done.
Seagulls winging to their clifftop home,
Tomorrow again the shore they will comb.
Refreshed in body and calmer in mind,
The empty beach my Pacific find.
There's a sense of peace one cannot describe,
Tho the solitude is there for us all to imbibe.

Ruth Robinson

ICEBERG

*(ME refers to Myalgic Encephalomyalopathy,
a long-term disabling condition)*

Me.
An iceberg.
Carved, carved, cut,
from the society that bore me.
Away. Adrift. Cast aside. In a boundless sea.
Nothing on the horizons.
Limitless yet utterly limited, I drift.
No force of my own. Subject to whim
and winds and unseen tide. I drift.
And, as an iceberg, much is hidden, concealed,
dangerously low. The Tears. Great cursing, coursing flows
that ebb, and tide, and pour again. Hidden. Apart . . . from life.
And hidden anger. At me, At ME. At 'this is *not* me!'
For I am more. Surely I am more. Hidden depths.
Pursuing the hidden depths. Riding the tides
of storm that sweep me, ME as my world.
Looking, delving, diving, deeper. To the depths of myself.
My soul. My being. My reason to live.
For *surely* I am more?
Surely, when unwholed below, and sinking, surely
I still live?
I am more. I am. Great unplumbed depths of me.
Uncharted, unexplored. Beckoning, dreadful sheer.
Blue-green ice. Sheer falls. Light play, and the light delves deep,
deep into my soul. Lightening me. Enlightening me. Bidding me
hold on. Go deeper.
Much deeper. Much more to go.
Inside me. Below ME.
Holding me, enfolding me.
Reassured,
I enter the floe.

Carrie Thomas

COTTON WOOL SKIES

Lazy summer days
Skies of blue, white and gold
feeling good cotton wool clouds
float over the wood
sailing on by without a care
I look for a sign but it's not there.
I want to sing
I want to dance
swirling round as in a trance
my imagination runs riot
Secret paths spread across the sky
hid away places I picture faces
soft winds spread the clouds
dispersing them in all directions
glimpses of sunlight pure warm
pale blue skies like silken gown
wrapped around those Heavenly clouds
perfume flows from scented flowers
air bitter-sweet, butterflies like
Fairies flutter to and fro
Bumblebees here to tease
feeling sleepy mind of dreams
A joy to treasure reaches out
beyond measure my cotton wool skies.

V Anderson

NATURE'S WONDER

Sweeping, soaring, dipping, diving,
Up and down the sky they go.
In formation, perfect timing,
One continuous ebb and flow.

Making patterns, one with Nature,
Just as if they've trained for years.
Not one crash, or smash or drop out,
Everyone devoid of fears.

Now, you're thinking, she's describing
Men performing with great skill
It's a team of brave Red Arrows
If you do - the answer's nil!

It's the common starlings, waving
In their acrobatic flight
Such a perfect joy to see them
- Nature's wonder? Yes, you're right!

Gwen Tipper

SUNLIGHT ON SEA SPRAY

A spring dawning has glory all its own
as sunlight assorts her own box of gems
to bejewel the tranquillity of sea,
from beach to horizon an immense plane
shows morning light racing unentrammelled.

Under swooping cries from gliding gulls
the vast blue pattern changes subtly
overlaying intense ultramarine,
splashing a canvas of glittering stars
highlighting dawn's polished diamond light.

Ridges of shining shingle at the waves' edge
are rich in foam-white glistening water
crackling the multigrained stones into sand
as the sun gains height, dazzling and glinting,
whilst small waves incessantly flow shorewards.

A freshening breeze adds to the motion,
a surface tide rustles this huge stretched sheen
of sunlit silk all a-shimmer in daylight.
Venetian waters seem, but slim bracelets
to this ocean's crown and necklace of pearls.

Dennis Marshall

AUTUMN DAYS

A walk through the wood is enchanting,
With fairy glades and imps in the trees.
Pictures are formed from twisted ivy,
From the mind, stories burst forth to tease.

Moorhen and ducks on the water skit,
In the shallows the fish catch the eye;
Peace abounds and contentment fills me,
'Oh if only,' thoughts bring forth a sigh.

The sun sets early, the birds still stir,
Shadows lengthen in a rosy glow;
The sun's rays deepen, the sky turns gold
And again peace settles on the show.

In the half light more pictures we see,
Shadows dance on the water and gleam;
The leaves flutter and sway to the tune,
Grotesque shapes in the trees form a theme.

As dusk falls, we walk home briskly,
In the warmth and comfort we then dine,
Well fed, relaxed, we've time to reflect
How fantasy and nature combine.

Janet Bowen

THE HAVEN

Now foxgloves bloom in stately ranks
Crowing the mossy fern-decked banks
Where earlier snowdrops overspread
Promise of all that lay ahead.
Primroses followed each dainty bloom
Scenting the air of this lovely combe;
Next trespassing cuckoo boasts of nest
Where her single egg was laid to rest
Dog roses soon will open wide
Embroidering the hedges on either side;
Ivy-clad tree trunks reach to the sky
Ragged robins nod to each passer-by;
Twittering birds and gurgling stream
Dappled sunshine - an artist's dream!
A place wherein to stand and stare
To offer up a silent prayer
That his haven may ever last
Never to become a scene from the past!

Roselie Mills

THE BRISK AIR

Upon a crispy November night beneath the twinkling stars
the leaves are falling fast.
Geese flying in from the Arctic are calling each other upon the wing.
The evening song in and among the hedgerows the chorus does begin.
Of red sunsets, twigs snap underfoot.
Water bubbles in a glistening brook.
The stags break the silence with a clash of antlers.
A rolling carpet of heather covers the highland glen.
A pheasant in the undergrowth displays its tail feathers.
Rabbits emerge from their warrens and hiding holes
an alarm call breaks of the blackbird,
down vaults the vole to his river bank hole.
Spying noses sniff the air.
Summer's gone, winter's setting in upon the setting sun.
Squirrels forage to and fro looking for nuts they buried months ago
how they do this I'm flabbergasted, I guess I'll never, ever know.
The forests and woods are a patchwork quilt of reds, oranges, yellows
With a light frost the odd sprinkling of snow
I watch the seasons come and go.
The blossoming of the English rose and the cooing of the dove
Ah my summer love.
Cream teas on a hot summer's eve
Spent in the silvery light of moonbeams.

Jonathan Covington

WINTER THOUGHTS

Jackdaws, 'jacking', crows cawing,
Rooks so raucous, hear their cries.
Bare trees, branches like black lace
Against the December skies.

Winds blowing, cold rain falling
From ragged, black clouds, racing
Over the darkened skies,
This bleak winter I'm facing.

Sitting by the warm, log fire,
Hearing the storm fierce, outside
Then dipping into my book,
I let my thoughts slowly glide.

This season though here, cannot last,
And summer is approaching fast.

Rose-Marie Bonnevier

NATURE'S WONDERS

The way that the seasons unfold,
Warmth of summer and winter's cold,
In-between the delicate spring
And the glow that autumn leaves bring.
The morning birdsong from small throats
Issuing sounds of purest notes,
They fly around the rooftop eaves,
There to build bests of twigs and leaves.

Sun filters through the forest glade,
Making patterns in dappled shade.
Rough seas that give a fine display,
Scattering foaming, lacy spray,
Onto the rocks that staunchly stand
Amid surrounding golden sand.
Many wonders that Nature shows,
Our admiration grows and grows.

Lilian Owen

MEMORIES OF A HOME IN BRITTANY

From ev'ry place around this stone-walled home
I see the verdant green of fields and trees -
I know the scent of wild flow'rs on the breeze -
All this I see when hither I do come.

From garden lavender a dreamy scent -
Its purple gown in summer zephyrs bent.
On low stoned wall a lizard darts along!
I hear the cheerful chirp of birds in song.

I see the high blue skies with sails of white
Which drift across the vastness of its space
To light the glory of this lovely place -
I wonder in the magic of this sight!

Such memories this home has given me -
They'll be with me into eternity!

John Paget

LATE AUTUMN

From green to gold
   A slow, unhurried change
From warm to cold
   With clothes to rearrange.

Another ring to add
   To time's relentless flight
The stoat's coat so sad
   To turn to white.

The balding trees that shed
   Their curling leaves once more
The dying flowers that bred
   Such joy in summer's core
Now leave their seeds
   On leafy covered floor
To trust the ground
   That Nature feeds
For next year's waiting spring
   That wills her progeny to wing.

The quieting time of autumn's spell
   The resting from the summer's toil
The thanksgiving of the harvest bell
   The worm casts sleeping coil.

The combination of wind and rain
   Of light and dark
Of sun and ice and gentle pain
   Ensures the need for autumn's mark.

J Aldred

AS WINTER AWAKENS

Arms
Of silver frost
Are lifted
Towards
Blue sky.

Cups of crystalled
Seed heads
Open to
The sun.

Drifts of frozen
Grasses
Drape in
Static
Form

And the birds
Of early morning
Greet
A brand new
Day!

Lyn Sandford

WEATHER

The sun can scorch the ground until there's nothing green,
Yet gently its reflection will caress a placid stream.

With a field of corn, a whispering wind will play,
But when in turmoil, wind destroys anything in its way.

Snow can be a feather, floating silently to the ground,
Or like a vice, gripping, so nothing moves around.

The rain as a teardrop, will trickle down the window pane,
Or be a deluge beyond control, causing havoc once again.

Weather, do we really know?
Is it friend, or is it foe?

John Booth

DEEP IN THE WOOD

Deep in the wood the bluebells grow,
And there the windflowers softly blow,
The beech tree buds of amber sheen
Are opening to the clearest green,
On arching branches sweeping low.

A pearling drift whiter than snow,
In thorny hedge pale petals glow,
Star trailing lace dark trunks between,
Deep in the wood.

The present slips, the truth we know
That past and future come and go,
A thought, a sigh for what has been,
The dreamtime lost that once was seen,
Here where sweet song and beauty flow,
Deep in the wood.

Alice Rawlinson

THE WONDER OF YOU
(Dedicated to James Green)

I love the sun, the way it shines
I love the sea, and the way it smells.
I love the leaves that hang off the trees
I love the grass and the way it felt.

I love sitting down among the trees
Feeling relaxed with a clear mind.
I love it when you're with me
You make everything more beautiful I find.

If I had to choose my favourite thing
I would have to choose you,
You make the air smell fresher
And I love looking at you.

I love the way you taste
Love the way your skin feels
I love the way you sound
You make the world seem real.

You make me aware of the things around
You help me see things in a different way
You reinforce the trivial things
You make my life brighter every day.

Jodie McKane

JUNE

On wings of sleep the cuckoo's song,
From far away, comes soft but strong.
The misty hours like a bloom,
Unfold into a trembling tune
Of sparrows darting through the trees
And blue tits nesting in the eaves.

Along the hedge wild roses wait,
With crumpled petals, to awake.
The creatures of the night make way,
Down bolt or burrow, for the day.
The house has sailed, a tiny ark,
Safe through the raven plumes of dark.

Andria J Cooke

REPEATEDLY

Repeatedly I cast my hook
Where branches overhang the brook
Where leaves like pretty sail boats glide
Askance against the wherryside

An onomatopoeic bird
Above the murmuring stream is heard
Yet inattentive to her cry
Repeatedly I dab my fly

Now with my long days fishing through
Distinct I hear the same cuckoo

Repeatedly;

Repeatedly;

Repeatedly:

Maurice Ivor Birch

WHERE THE KINGFISHER DARTS

I know a place, where gentle hills
A green and peaceful valley form.
Where watchful trees give shade,
By silver lakes,
Where the kingfisher darts.

Oft times in quiet contemplation
I dream that I am there,
Standing among the watchful trees
By silver lakes,
Where the kingfisher darts.

The seasons enhance its loveliness
In a kaleidoscope of shadows and hues,
As the watchful trees disrobe,
By silver lakes,
Where the kingfisher darts.

I know a place,
Where my dreams become reality,
Shaded, beneath the watchful trees,
Standing, close by the silver lakes,
Waiting, to see the kingfisher dart.

Joan Thompson

MORNING

The early mist has shrouded all around
and friendly hedgerows, fields and trees are masked.
Too early yet, the sun has barely stirred
and songbirds quiet still waiting to be asked.

Then life it springs as sunshine filters through
the song of birds from tree and hedgerow shrill.
Another day of wonders now unfold
as Nature with surprises ever thrill.

The freshness of each day can lift your soul
and spread around for all to see and touch.
The fruitfulness of Nature at its best,
it makes us all so thankful for so much.

For morning air to breathe, and skies to see
a fresh new day of beauty fills the heart.
As new lambs romp and play so joyfully
and with light step another day you start.

Alan J Vincent

SONNET
(War, fruit and poetry)

This form is so elusive but so true,
The words are tempered, as of iron wrought
And this allows some meaning to come through.
Are people's feelings meaning worth a thought?
I've never come across this grace before,
Compression in a space must yield some fruit?
Creative energies are squashed in war,
But like the Bonsai pain must have its beauty.
As we writhe and twist around, our heart kept
Some little ball of roots below the ground
Our tiny, twisted branches groan unslept,
Containment and restriction violent found.
Restrictions seem so full of contradiction
Since limits set are limitless in diction.

Lucy Boyd

FAMINE

A pot-bellied child on our TV screen,
Limbs like sticks, an awful scene.
Its tired body and sad, round eyes,
Will no one listen to its cries?

More cry for food and help no doubt,
It's not their fault they've had a drought.
But someone, somewhere always moans,
leave them be, they're skin and bone.

They'll not live long so let them be,
You see I've got my family.
But they're the ones, who need the help,
Whose selfish ways will cause to yelp!

When others care and help with aid,
Those images so soon will fade.
For I have this dream of a better place,
Of a well fed child with a happy face.
But as I said, it's just a dream,
But, we all could make that better scene.

Tracey Davies

UNTITLED

Journeys can be near or far
You can travel by bus or by car
You can get to Spain by boat or plane
Journeys can be near or far.

To travel by plane across different countries
To work or visit the famous places
To go to war which we are afraid
Please get back home and peace is made.

Journeys can be near or far
Travel to families or friends from afar
Go round the corner to visit the shops
Or in a taxi or at a bus stop
Journeys can be near or far.

The services need to travel by road
They can use an ambucopter to pick up a load
The police have to check on people's speed
To make sure they are doing their deed
The fire engines need to rush through the traffic
It's hard work when it's busy or static
Journeys can be near or far.

Wayne Covell (9)

YOU ARE STILL THERE

You are still there wherever I am,
Showing me what to do,
A beautiful image you are,
Whenever the days are blue.

You are still there whenever the time,
Night or day,
In my late dreams you are,
Making me happy and gay.

Victoria Maguire (11)

THE NIGHT RIDER

Look the night rider is riding,
Silently he's gliding,
His steed gathers pace,
To win the race,
Not a sound or he will stop
Sniff the air and say,
'Something is here with us, we must be on our way.'

Then he will ride on,
Until the moon is gone,
But he'll be back,
When the sky is black.

The morning's here and he and his horse wait,
Till the sun shines on them to take them back through the gate.

Morag Boles (9)

BOYS

Boys, boys, make lots of noise!
Boys, boys, still play with their toys.
Boys, boys, they're such a pain
Boys, boys, they're just insane.

Lisa Dickson (13)

MEMORIES

I will remember the big school crowded
I will remember the children surrounded
I will miss teachers and Sparky the pet
But I will be leaving yet
In September
A day to remember.

I'm glad I'm leaving to be a grown-up at once
Have a party to jump up and bounce
Children moving on
So I'll be way gone
In September
A day to remember.

Niketa Booth (11)

THE PARK

With its wildlife running wild and free,
The park is a place I like to be,
The toddlers shout and kids do play,
I like to visit the park every day.

With the wonderful leaves that change each year,
In the park I have no fear,
The pigeons are always looking for food,
No one here is in a bad mood.

The elderly sit around and stare,
At the wonderful beauty that's displayed there,
Ducks swim and flap happily in the pond,
Everyone has an almighty bond.

The park is my favourite place to go,
For there I have no evil foe,
The beauty is wonderful in the glimmering sun,
Nobody goes without fun.

So come on now and join in with me,
And see how much fun this can be,
There is so much to do in this beautiful place,
You'll never see a miserable face.

Matthew Allan (12)

SPRING

Nature's secrets finally begin
Blossoms grow in the beautiful days of spring.
Spring power makes things grow, not much dies in spring.
Quietness as wild animals run in daylight and darkness.
The animal hunters look for food in the warmer nights.
Everything is alive once more.

Jake Norfolk

HAUNTED HOUSE

Bone chilling nightmares
Ghastly calls,
Creaking floorboards,
Cracks in the walls!

Horror movies
Flying popcorn,
Shivering bodies -
Darkness is born.

Unknown shadows
Lurking ghosts,
'Stay away from this area', it says
On signposts.

Headless gnomes
On the gardens' dark grass -
Trees with eyes
That watch you as you pass!

'Cling, clang!'
Goes the teeth of a flower.
Watch out for that wire -
Oops! There goes the power!

'Shh!' There's a whisper -
What could it be?
How do you know?
You can't see.

Creak, Creak!
As you walk down the hall,
You see something in the corner -
Don't sprint - you might fall.

Turn around.
Don't peep behind.
Search for the nearest exit
That you can find.

Nothing,
There's not one door.
Feel the trembling boards
Of the floor!

You start to worry -
Can you feel your fear
As the shadow of a person
Appears to be near?

You've bumped into something -
You're heart beats like a drum!
You look up with fear -
Oh look! It's your mum!

Rachel Barnes (11)

THE GYPSY DANCE

Around in a circle they wildly prance,
Leaping and singing the words to their dance.
Lovely bright petticoats red, blue and green,
In the big crowd of bodies, are all that are seen.

They keep on dancing late into the night,
The stars come out, the moon shines bright.
They eat chicken from the bone with a little rice
And throw the left-overs to the mice.

The night turns black and the wind is so cold,
They start to tire, with their big hoops of gold.
The camp fire glows, a mysterious red
And they skip to their caravans and go to bed.

Jessica Woodley (10)

CATS' CHORUS

All seven cats lined up in a row,
Open mouthed and ready to go.
The conductor is ready,
His baton held high,
The cats are performing more than a sigh.
The cats start to sing,
In a very high pitch,
They stamp their feet
To the rhythm of the beat.
All that comes out is a squeaky miaow
And all that was left was to take a big bow.

Perdita Palmer (10)

I WOULD LIKE TO BE A GULL

I would like to be a gull
Flying up in the sky
higher than high.
I would love to be a gull . . .

Watching the sunset go down
behind the clouds.
Feeling the soft sea spray on my wings
I would see the most wonderful things . . .

As I swoop down to retrieve a silver fish,
it wriggles about in my mouth
and tries to get out.
But I would hold tight and swallow it whole.

Then I'd fly home to my nest
and rest.

Daisy Marsh (10)

A Ship Sails

A radiant ship, of immortal beauty
Came sailing towards us, extremely swervily
It was fiery and gleamed in the sun,
And it was a real pageant for everyone.
It glimmered like an opal, and shone like a jewel.
And went swiftly windward towards the town of Ewell.

So this is the tale of my sweet memory,
Which shall stay in my heart way out at sea.

Georgia Pritchard (9)

DREAMS

They say a dream is supposed to mean,
That there's something you need to know,
But my dreams don't mean anything
They're really weird though,

I go to bed, and my weary head
works overtime as I sleep,
going over previous dreams
before I take a great, big leap.
into a world with a fantasy theme
that all looks so real and new,
but I fail to realise the obvious thing -
that in fact it's all so untrue

Tanya Jade Johnson (11)

MY PARENTS ARE THE GREATEST!

My parents are the greatest,
They deserve some money,
For laughing at my appalling jokes,
The ones that are not funny!

My parents are the greatest,
Because despite the stress and strife,
They've been a fantastic influence to me
And put a good shape to my life!

My parents are the greatest,
My dad always watches me play,
He follows my team all over the place
Even on a rainy day!

My parents are the greatest,
My mum is always keen,
To give me a cuddle when we watch TV,
Even though I'm now 16!

My parents are the greatest,
Though looking back in retrospect,
They've done all this, worked so hard
Yet I gave them little respect!

So Mum and Dad, I want to say,
That if I have some kids - one day,
Then I will be a parent too
And my best effort will be based on you!

Other people say their folks are great
But I just come out in smiles,
'How can that be?' I have to ask,
Cos mine are the best by miles!

Martin Doyle

MIST-DEMEANOURS

Eerie, still, - like ghosts:
Searching . . .

Curling promiscuous fingers under clothing.
Breathing white swirling fogs into valleys -
Waiting for breezes.

Dank, dark, chilling . . .
Coiling scarves of chiffon 'round trunks in woods.

- A clinging to hair and hoods . . .

A fineness of drizzle hanging low beneath
Skies of dropped and cloudy imagery
Covering damply the greasy run of roads.

Where cattle surrounded by whispers
Blow their hot steamy breaths
Into fields beyond cities
Onto people walking on pavements.

P J Harris

UNEXPECTED

Suitcase packed
Case lid
Popped open
Mighty force
Shot contents
Across room
Landed in cat loo
Flying shoe
Broke windowpane
Landed in lane
Hit postman
Who shouted out in pain
Train to catch
Half-past two
Must not be late
For my holiday date
Round corner
Taxi came
That was late.

Mary Miller

TIME TO SAY GOODBYE

Facing up to your very worst fear,
The dread of your dearest's death.
Emotions build as the end is near,
Could this be their very last breath?

It doesn't help, whatever you say,
Or whatever you try to do.
They just deteriorate day by day,
And could anyone possibly help you?

How do you let them go?
How can you say goodbye?
Especially when they don't know,
That they're about to die.

How do you just carry on -
Without them, when they've gone?

Lynne Doyle

ICON
(For Darryl)

It's strange to find you staring back at me:
From glossy magazines that practised smile;
Each time my train pulls into Gloucester Road
Your three foot grin beams down across the aisle.
Some nights you flit across my TV screen,
Your twinkling eye winks down from passing bus;
You find fresh sparkle for the camera lens,
A face like yours could even sell a truss.
Those fashion shots are not the you we know -
You're different in the family snaps we keep -
You can project an image just for show,
But does the world still know you when you sleep?
As fashion icon you work hard, it's true -
But as a son we see a different you.

Patrick Osada

THE GENTLE TYRANT

I have a cat
named Silver Surprise.
Mum's a Chinchilla Persian,
Dad's a Black Alley.
He was the result
of an unplanned pregnancy.
'More of a *shock,*'
said Glenda, his breeder!

He is so gorgeous -
black stripes on soft, dense silver undercoat,
spectacular striated tail,
waving banner-like in greeting,
russet-tipped nose,
round, liquid-green eyes
ringed by dark eye-liner,
elegantly downward-curving silver whiskers,
soft, gentle purr,
'Incredibly beautiful,' people say.

He knows so well
how to get his way -
prowls and weaves around, talking the while.
(At a cat show, the TV reporter asked,
'Is yours the one who talks?')
He's developed 'getting in the way'
into a fine art!

People look into his eyes,
his trustful, beguiling face,
and *smile!* 'So laid back,' says the vet,
as she gives him a cuddle.

Yes, he is a tyrant,
but would I be without him?
No - for even on my darkest days,
he makes me *smile*.

Maria-Christina

NATURAL HABITAT

You stand and pose but for awhile
To rest your wings shown off in style
You search around for friends in flight
Soaring way above the heights
You sing among the berry bush
While picking at its fruit
You stand so proud and colourful
In your pretty suit
You preen your feathers once again
To get ready for the flight
To go and join the rest of them
Up there in great height

Dorreen Read

REQUIEM FOR DALI

Elephants march the time of death
A knell from Dali's brush
With legs, the threads of time
Upon the spiders' webs.

Into the sudden hush
The tiger springs her claws
Whilst she with tender lip
Unto the plot enjoys.

Into the march of time
The Dali master paints,
Whilst ants trace subtle grace
And treads the tiger trance.

The end comes next to her,
The mistress of his muse,
Where I, with sudden note,
Condemn the loss of time.

Richard Cole

SUBMISSIONS INVITED
SOMETHING FOR EVERYONE

POETRY NOW 2002 - Any subject,
any style, any time.

WOMENSWORDS 2002 - Strictly women,
have your say the female way!

STRONGWORDS 2002 - Warning!
Age restriction, must be between 16-24,
opinionated and have strong views.
(Not for the faint-hearted)

All poems no longer than 30 lines.
Always welcome! No fee!
Cash Prizes to be won!

Mark your envelope (eg *Poetry Now*) *2002*
Send to:
Forward Press Ltd
Remus House, Coltsfoot Drive,
Peterborough, PE2 9JX

**OVER £10,000 POETRY PRIZES
TO BE WON!**

Judging will take place in October 2002